REVISED EDITION

59 SONGS FOR WEDDINGS AND RECEPTIONS
CLASSICAL/TRADITIONAL • POP/ROCK CLASSICS • BROADWAY • STANDARDS • CONTEMPORARY CHRISTIAN

ISBN 978-0-7935-4096-9

7777 W. BLUEMOUND RD. P.O. BOX 13819 MILWAUKEE, WI 53213

For all works contained herein:
Unauthorized copying, arranging, adapting, recording, Internet posting, public performance,
or other distribution of the printed music in this publication is an infringement of copyright.
Infringers are liable under the law.

Visit Hal Leonard Online at
www.halleonard.com

Contents

All Good Gifts	62
All I Ask of You	57
All the Way	90
Always	119
Annie's Song	124
Ave Maria (Bach/Gounod)	5
Ave Maria (Schubert)	8
Be Thou My Vision	12
Bist du bei mir (You Are With Me)	22
Dank sei Dir, Herr (Thanks Be to God)	17
Du Ring an meinem Finger (The Ring on My Finger)	26
Endless Love	134
Entreat Me Not to Leave Thee	30
The First Time Ever I Saw Your Face	131
Fly Me to the Moon	93
God Causes All Things to Grow	206
God Knew That I Needed You	210
The Greatest of These	68
Grow Old With Me	142
Here, There and Everywhere	147
Household of Faith	214
How Beautiful	218
I Could Write a Book	96
I Will	150
I Will Be Here	226
If	153
If You Could See What I See	199
In My Life	156
Jesu, Joy of Man's Desiring	37
Just the Way You Are	159
Laudate Dominum	42
Let It Be Me	166
Longer	174
The Lord's Prayer	47
Love of My Life	232
Love Will Be Our Home	236
My Place Is with You	243
Panis Angelicus	52
Parent's Prayer (Let Go of Two)	248
The Promise (I'll Never Say Goodbye)	99
Shine on Us	252
Someone Like You	72
Starting Here, Starting Now	102
Sunrise, Sunset	76
This Day	262
This Is the Day	266
Till There Was You	86
Time After Time	105
Unexpected Song	81
Walk Hand in Hand	108
The Way You Look Tonight	111
We've Only Just Begun	171
Wedding Song (There Is Love)	178
When I Fall in Love	114
Where There Is Love	257
With a Song in My Heart	116
You Are So Beautiful	186
You Needed Me	189
You Raise Me Up	194

CONTENTS BY CATEGORY

Classical/Traditional

5	AVE MARIA	J.S. BACH/CHARLES GOUNOD
8	AVE MARIA	FRANZ SCHUBERT
12	BE THOU MY VISION	arr. RICHARD WALTERS
22	BIST DU BEI MIR (You Are With Me)	GOTTFRIED HEINRICH STÖLZEL (PREVIOUSLY ATTRIBUTED TO J.S. BACH)
17	DANK SEI DIR, HERR (Thanks Be to God)	SIEGFRIED OCHS (PREVIOUSLY ATTRIBUTED TO GEORGE FRIDERIC HANDEL)
26	DU RING AN MEINEM FINGER (The Ring on My Finger)	ROBERT SCHUMANN
30	ENTREAT ME NOT TO LEAVE THEE	CHARLES GOUNOD
37	JESU, JOY OF MAN'S DESIRING	J.S. BACH
42	LAUDATE DOMINUM	WOLFGANG AMADEUS MOZART
47	THE LORD'S PRAYER	ALBERT HAY MALOTTE
52	PANIS ANGELICUS	CÉSAR FRANCK

Broadway

62	ALL GOOD GIFTS	FROM *GODSPELL*
57	ALL I ASK OF YOU	FROM *THE PHANTOM OF THE OPERA*
68	THE GREATEST OF THESE	FROM *PHILEMON*
72	SOMEONE LIKE YOU	FROM *JEKYLL & HYDE*
76	SUNRISE, SUNSET	FROM *FIDDLER ON THE ROOF*
86	TILL THERE WAS YOU	FROM *THE MUSIC MAN*
81	UNEXPECTED SONG	FROM *SONG & DANCE*

Standards

RECORDED BY (AMONG OTHERS):

90	ALL THE WAY	FRANK SINATRA
93	FLY ME TO THE MOON	TONY BENNETT
96	I COULD WRITE A BOOK	FRANK SINATRA
99	THE PROMISE (I'll Never Say Goodbye)	MELISSA MANCHESTER
102	STARTING HERE, STARTING NOW	BARBRA STREISAND
105	TIME AFTER TIME	FRANK SINATRA
108	WALK HAND IN HAND	GERRY AND THE PACEMAKERS; ANDY WILLIAMS
111	THE WAY YOU LOOK TONIGHT	FRANK SINATRA; TONY BENNETT
114	WHEN I FALL IN LOVE	NAT "KING" COLE
116	WITH A SONG IN MY HEART	PERRY COMO

CONTENTS BY CATEGORY

Pop/Rock Classics

Page	Title	Recorded by:
119	Always	Michael W. Smith
124	Annie's Song	John Denver
134	Endless Love	Diana Ross and Lionel Richie
131	The First Time Ever I Saw Your Face	Roberta Flack
142	Grow Old With Me	John Lennon; Mary Chapin Carpenter
147	Here, There and Everywhere	The Beatles
150	I Will	The Beatles
153	If	Bread
156	In My Life	The Beatles
159	Just the Way You Are	Billy Joel
166	Let It Be Me	The Everly Brothers
174	Longer	Dan Fogelberg
178	Wedding Song (There Is Love)	Paul Stookey
171	We've Only Just Begun	The Carpenters
186	You Are So Beautiful	Joe Cocker
189	You Needed Me	Anne Murray
194	You Raise Me Up	Josh Groban

Contemporary Christian

Page	Title	Recorded by:
206	God Causes All Things to Grow	Steve Green
210	God Knew That I Needed You	Dick and Mel Tunney
214	Household of Faith	Steve and Marijean Green
218	How Beautiful	Twila Paris
226	I Will Be Here	Steven Curtis Chapman
199	If You Could See What I See	Geoff Moore & The Distance
232	Love of My Life	Michael W. Smith
236	Love Will Be Our Home	Sandi Patty
243	My Place Is with You	Clay Crosse
248	Parent's Prayer (Let Go of Two)	Steven Curtis Chapman
252	Shine on Us	Phillips, Craig & Dean
262	This Day	Portrait of Grace
266	This Is the Day	Scott Wesley Brown
257	Where There Is Love	Scott Wesley Brown; Phill McHugh

Ave Maria

CHARLES GOUNOD
Adapted from the Prelude in C Major by J.S. BACH

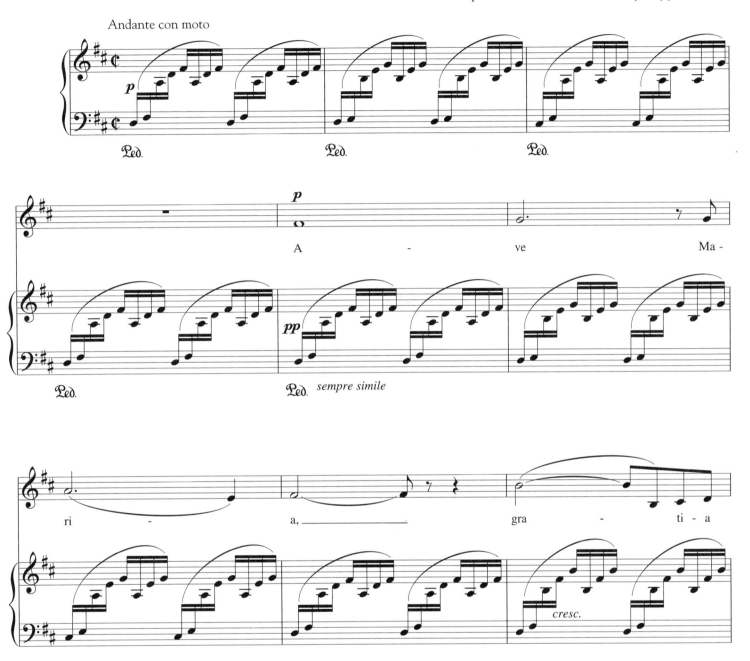

Ave Maria

FRANZ SCHUBERT

* *Normally, at a wedding, only sing the first verse.*

Copyright © 2002 by HAL LEONARD CORPORATION
International Copyright Secured   All Rights Reserved

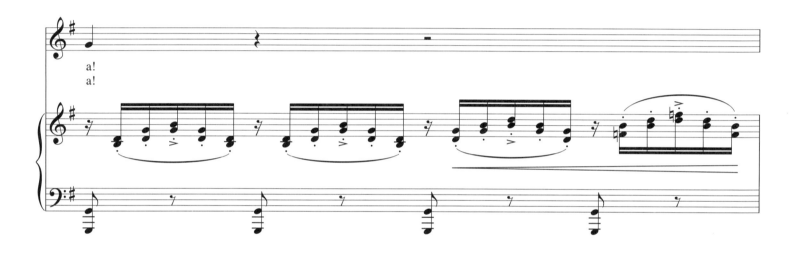

Be Thou My Vision

for Steve

Ancient Irish
Translated by Mary E. Byrne, 1905
Versified by Eleanor H. Hull, 1912

Traditional Irish Melody
Arranged by RICHARD WALTERS

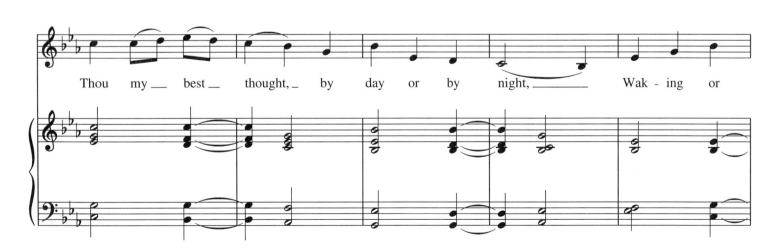

Copyright © 1993 by HAL LEONARD CORPORATION
International Copyright Secured   All Rights Reserved

16

* From here to the end may be either *piano* or *forte,* depending on the singer's best attributes.

Dank sei Dir, Herr
(Thanks Be to God)

SIEGFRIED OCHS*
(Previously attributed to HANDEL)

*Siegfried Ochs (1858-1929) claimed to have discovered an aria by Handel, and to have made an arrangement of the piece, which was published and became well-known. Closer research has revealed that this is actually an original composition by Ochs.

Copyright © 1992 by HAL LEONARD CORPORATION
International Copyright Secured   All Rights Reserved

Bist du bei mir
(You Are with Me)

GOTTFRIED HEINRICH STÖLZEL
(Previously attributed to J.S. BACH)

Copyright © 1992 by HAL LEONARD CORPORATION
International Copyright Secured   All Rights Reserved

Du Ring an meinem Finger
(The Ring on My Finger)

ADALBERT von CHAMISSO

ROBERT SCHUMANN

Copyright © 2003 by HAL LEONARD CORPORATION
International Copyright Secured   All Rights Reserved

Entreat Me Not to Leave Thee
(Song of Ruth)

From the Book of Ruth 1:16-17

CHARLES GOUNOD

Copyright © 1992 by HAL LEONARD CORPORATION
International Copyright Secured   All Rights Reserved

Because of length, a singer may choose to perform just verse one.

Laudate Dominum
from VESPERAE SOLENNES

WOLFGANG AMADEUS MOZART

Lau - da -

gratefully dedicated to my friend John Charles Thomas

The Lord's Prayer

ALBERT HAY MALOTTE

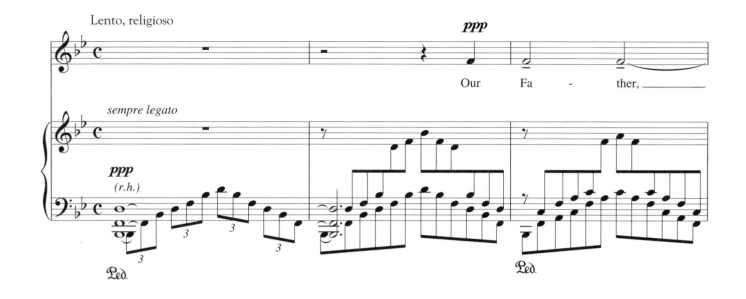
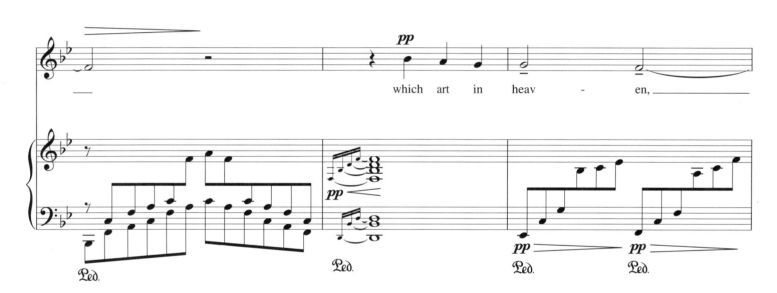

Copyright © 1935 (Renewed) by G. Schirmer, Inc. (ASCAP)
International Copyright Secured   All Rights Reserved
Reprinted by Permission

Panis Angelicus

CÉSAR FRANCK

All I Ask of You
from THE PHANTOM OF THE OPERA

Music by ANDREW LLOYD WEBBER
Lyrics by CHARLES HART
Additional Lyrics by RICHARD STILGOE

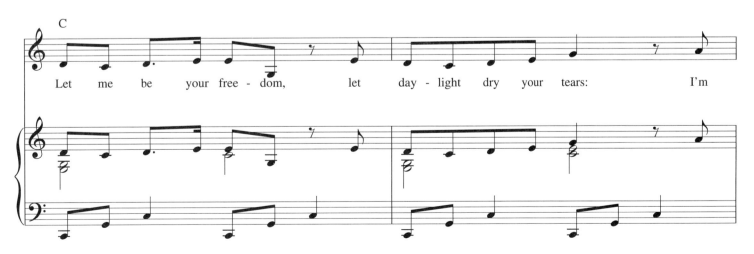

© Copyright 1986 Andrew Lloyd Webber licensed to The Really Useful Group Ltd.
International Copyright Secured   All Rights Reserved

All Good Gifts
from the Musical GODSPELL

Music by STEPHEN SCHWARTZ
Lyrics by MATTHIAS CLAUDIUS (1782)
Translated by JANE M. CAMPBELL (1861)

The Greatest of These
from PHILEMON

Words and Music by TOM JONES
and HARVEY SCHMIDT

Someone Like You
from JEKYLL & HYDE

Words by LESLIE BRICUSSE
Music by FRANK WILDHORN

Copyright © 1990 Stage And Screen Music, Ltd. (BMI), Cherry Lane Music Publishing Company, Inc. (ASCAP),
Dimensional Music Of 1091 (ASCAP), Les Etoiles De La Musique (ASCAP) and Scaramanga Music, Inc. (ASCAP)
Worldwide Rights for Stage And Screen Music, Ltd. Administered by Cherry River Music Co.
Worldwide Rights for Les Etoiles De La Musique and Scaramanga Music, Inc. Administered by Cherry Lane Music Publishing Company, Inc.
International Copyright Secured   All Rights Reserved

Unexpected Song
from SONG & DANCE

Music by ANDREW LLOYD WEBBER
Lyrics by DON BLACK

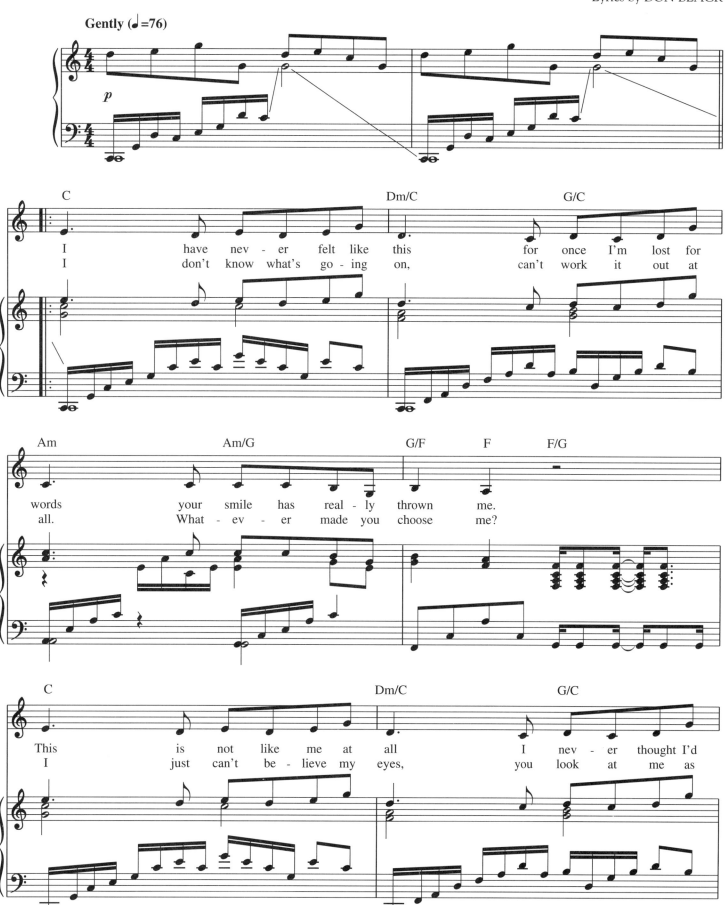

© Copyright 1978, 1982 Andrew Lloyd Webber licensed to The Really Useful Group Ltd.
International Copyright Secured   All Rights Reserved

Till There Was You
from Meredith Willson's THE MUSIC MAN

By MEREDITH WILLSON

All the Way
from the film THE JOKER IS WILD

Words by SAMMY CAHN
Music by JAMES VAN HEUSEN
Arranged by HANK POWELL

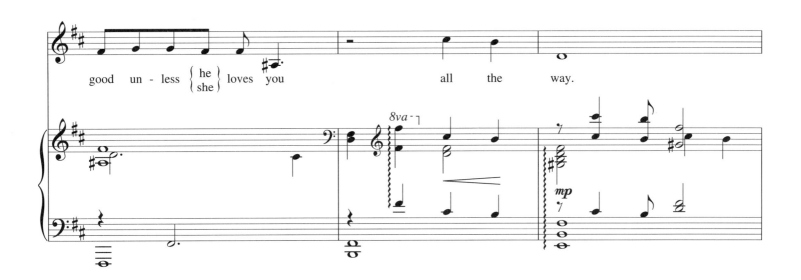

Copyright © 1957 (Renewed) Maraville Music Corp.
All Rights Reserved   Used by Permission

Fly Me to the Moon
(In Other Words)

Words and Music by BART HOWARD
Arranged by HANK POWELL

TRO - © Copyright 1954 (Renewed) Hampshire House Publishing Corp., New York, NY
International Copyright Secured
All Rights Reserved Including Public Performance For Profit
Used by Permission

I Could Write a Book
from PAL JOEY

Words by LORENZ HART
Music by RICHARD RODGERS
Arranged by BRIAN DEAN

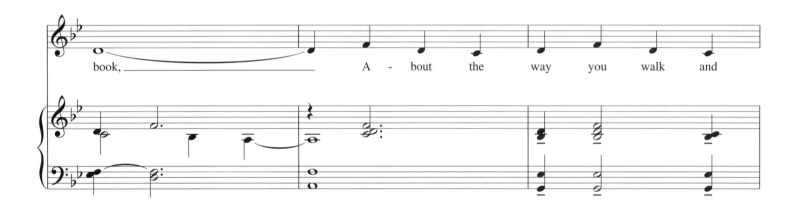
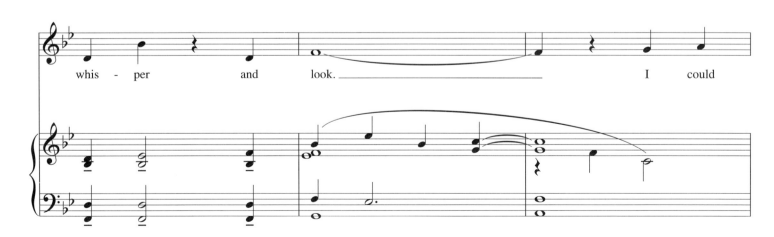

Copyright © 1940 (Renewed) by Chappell & Co.
Rights for the Extended Renewal Term in the U.S. Controlled by Williamson Music and WB Music Corp. o/b/o The Estate Of Lorenz Hart
International Copyright Secured   All Rights Reserved

The Promise
(I'll Never Say Goodbye)
Theme from the Universal Motion Picture THE PROMISE

Words by ALAN and MARILYN BERGMAN
Music by DAVID SHIRE

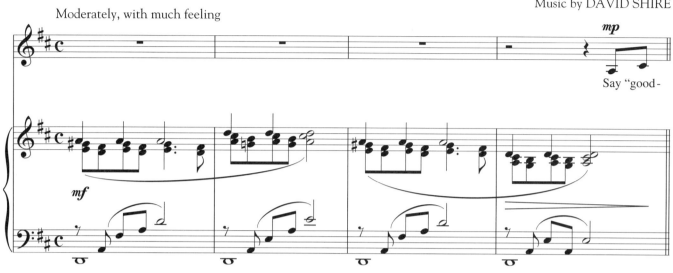

Copyright © 1978 USI A MUSIC PUBLISHING and USI B MUSIC PUBLISHING
All Rights for USI A MUSIC PUBLISHING Controlled and Administered by UNIVERSAL MUSIC CORP.
All Rights for USI B MUSIC PUBLISHING Controlled and Administered by SONGS OF UNIVERSAL, INC.
All Rights Reserved Used by Permission

*Cue notes optional 2nd time

Starting Here, Starting Now

Words by RICHARD MALTBY JR.
Music by DAVID SHIRE

Time After Time
from the Metro-Goldwyn-Mayer Picture IT HAPPENED IN BROOKLYN

Words by SAMMY CAHN
Music by JULE STYNE
Arranged by RICHARD WALTERS

Copyright © 1947 (Renewed) Sands Music Corp.
All Rights Reserved   Used by Permission

Walk Hand in Hand

Words and Music by
JOHNNY COWELL
Arranged by JOEL K. BOYD

Copyright © 1956 (Renewed) by Embassy Music Corporation (BMI)
International Copyright Secured   All Rights Reserved
Reprinted by Permission

110

When I Fall in Love

Words by EDWARD HEYMAN
Music by VICTOR YOUNG

Always

Words and Music by GARY CHAPMAN and
MICHAEL W. SMITH

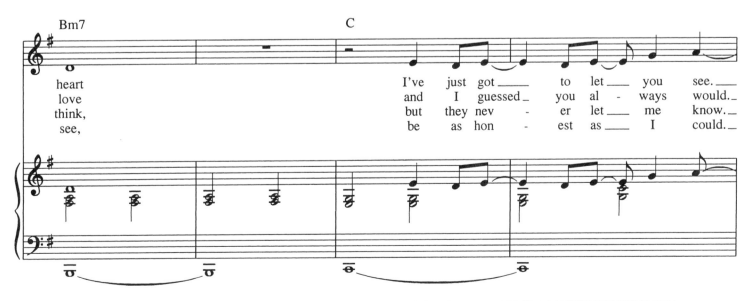

© 1981 MEADOWGREEN MUSIC COMPANY and PARAGON MUSIC (ASCAP) (Admin. by BRENTWOOD-BENSON MUSIC PUBLISHING, INC.)
MEADOWGREEN MUSIC COMPANY Admin. by EMI CMG PUBLISHING
All Rights Reserved   Used by Permission

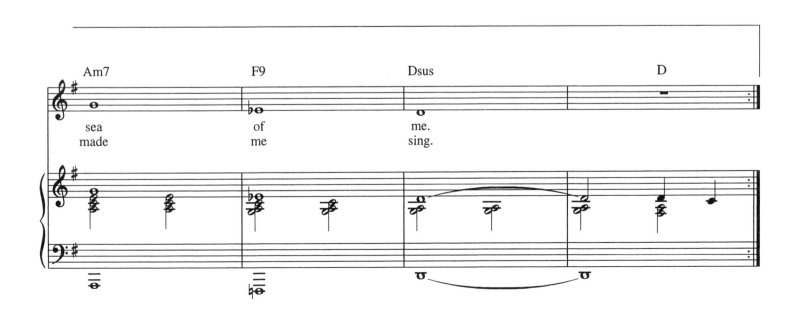

Annie's Song

Words and Music by JOHN DENVER
Arranged by RICHARD WALTERS

Copyright © 1974 Cherry Lane Music Publishing Company, Inc. (ASCAP)
Copyright Renewed and Assigned to Anna Kate Deutschendorf, Zachary Deutschendorf and Jesse Belle Denver in the U.S.
All Rights for Anna Kate Deutschendorf and Zachary Deutschendorf Administered by Cherry Lane Music Publishing Company, Inc.
All Rights for Jesse Belle Denver Administered by WB Music Corp.
International Copyright Secured   All Rights Reserved

The First Time Ever I Saw Your Face

Words and Music by
EWAN MacCOLL

Endless Love

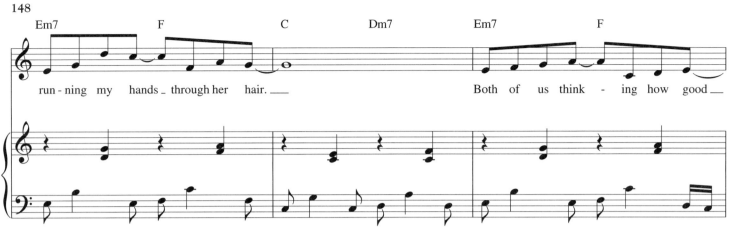
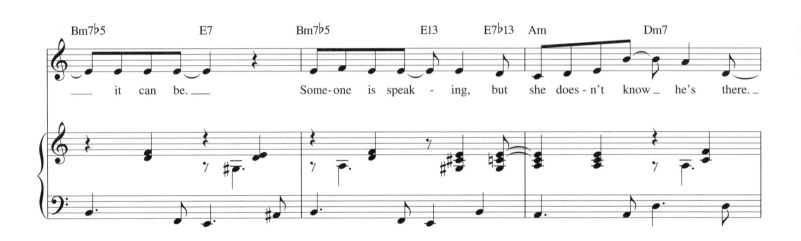

If

Words and Music by
DAVID GATES

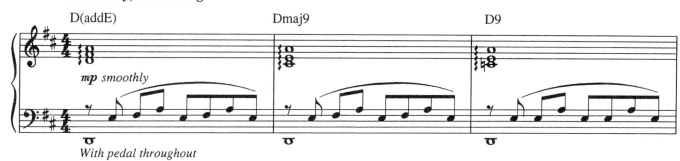
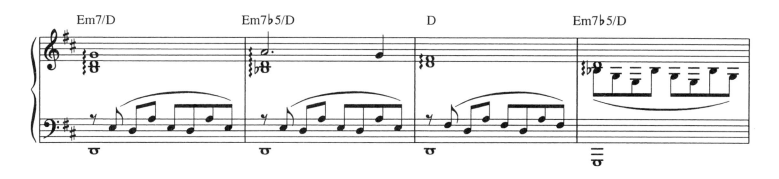
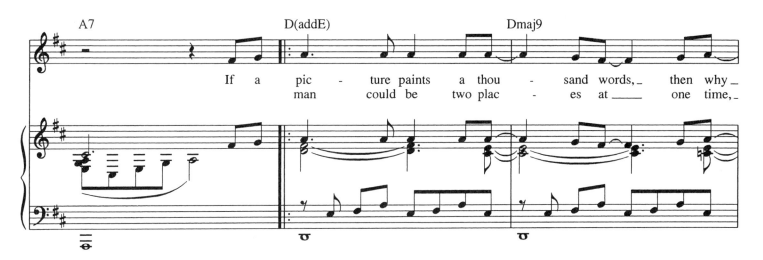
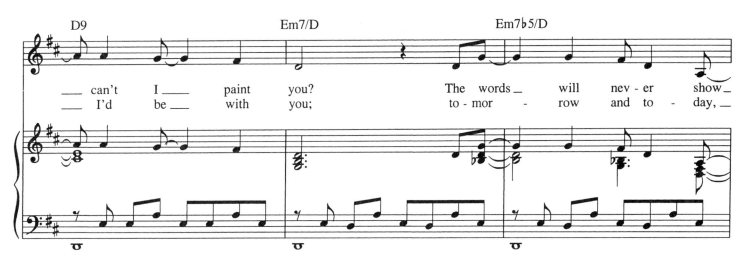

Copyright © 1971 Sony/ATV Music Publishing LLC
Copyright Renewed
All Rights Administered by Sony/ATV Music Publishing LLC, 8 Music Square West, Nashville, TN 37203
International Copyright Secured All Rights Reserved

We've Only Just Begun

Words and Music by ROGER NICHOLS
and PAUL WILLIAMS

Copyright © 1970 IRVING MUSIC, INC.
Copyright Renewed
All Rights Reserved   Used by Permission

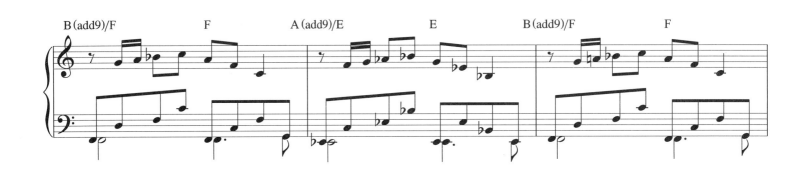

Wedding Song
(There Is Love)

Words and Music by
PAUL STOOKEY

Slowly, in 2

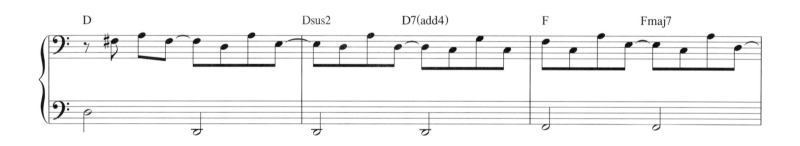

He is

Copyright © 1971 Public Domain Foundation, Inc.
Copyright Renewed 1999
Administered by Music & Media International, Inc.
International Copyright Secured All Rights Reserved

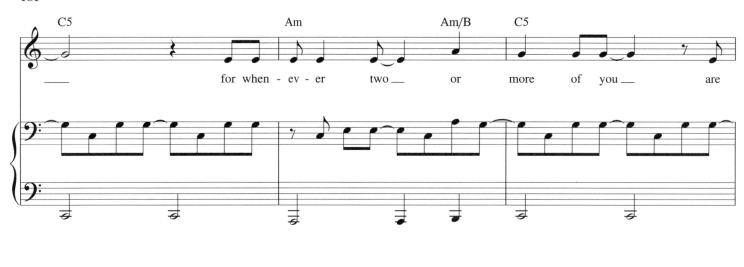
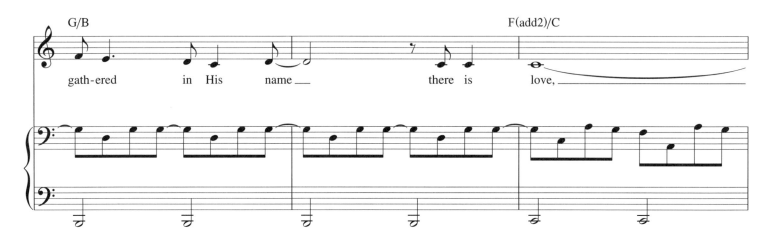

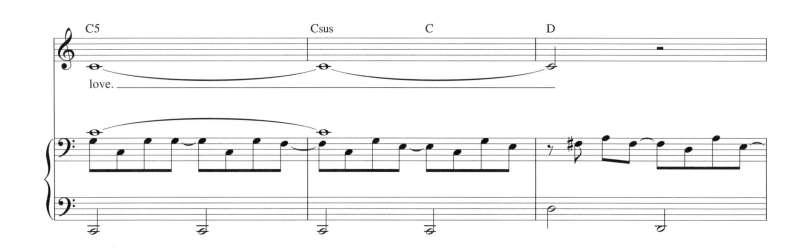

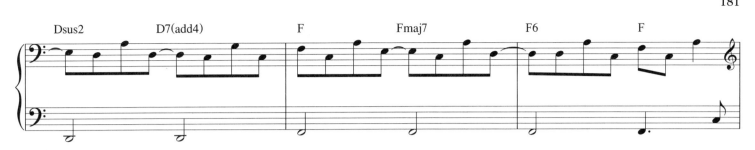
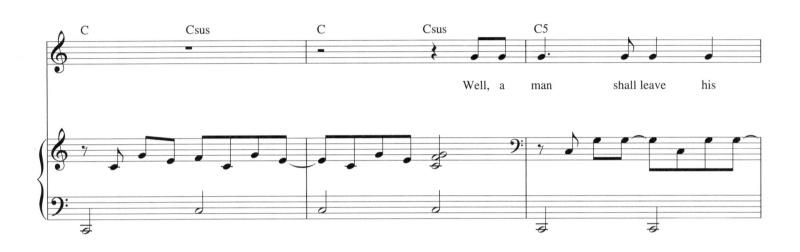

You Needed Me

Words and Music by
RANDY GOODRUM

Copyright © 1975, 1978 by Chappell & Co. and Ironside Music
Copyright Renewed
All Rights Administered by Chappell & Co.
International Copyright Secured   All Rights Reserved

You Raise Me Up

Words and Music by BRENDAN GRAHAM
and ROLF LOVLAND

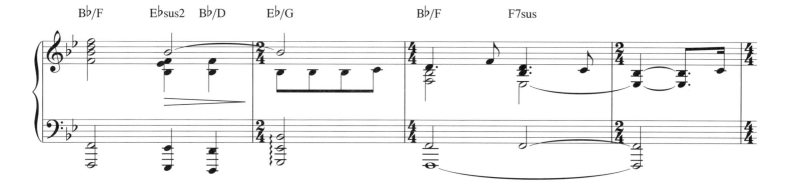
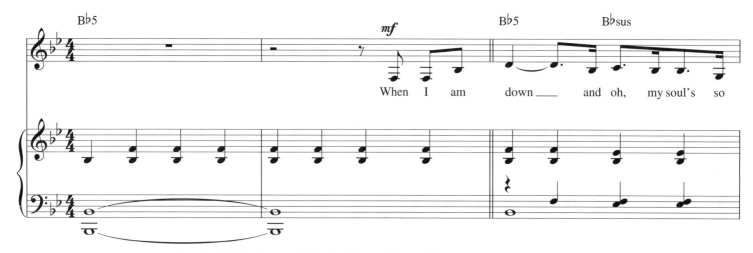

Copyright © 2002 by Peermusic (UK) Ltd. and Universal Music Publishing, A Division of Universal Music AS
All Rights for Peermusic (UK) Ltd. in the United States Controlled and Administered by Peermusic III, Ltd.
All Rights for Universal Music Publishing, A Division of Universal Music AS in the United States and Canada Controlled and Administered by
Universal - PolyGram International Publishing, Inc.
International Copyright Secured   All Rights Reserved

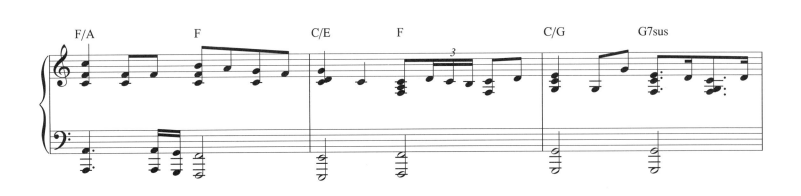
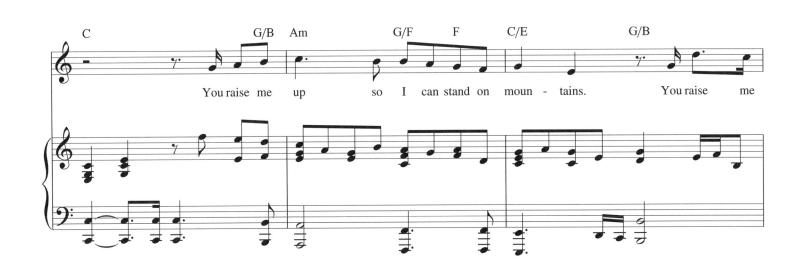

*This repeat may be omitted.

God Causes All Things To Grow

Words and Music by STEVEN CURTIS CHAPMAN
and STEVE GREEN

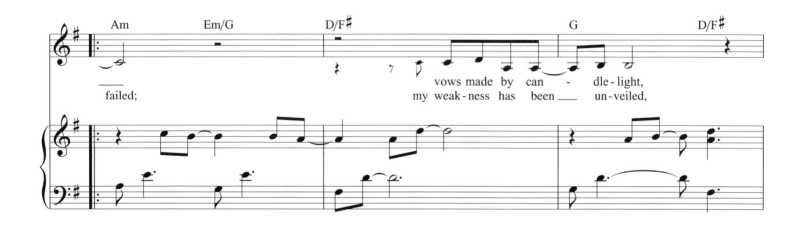
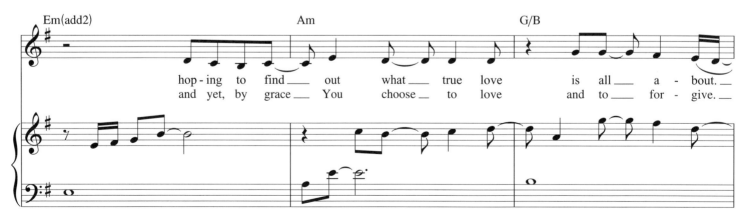

© 1994 BIRDWING MUSIC (ASCAP), SPARROW SONG (BMI), STEVE GREEN MUSIC (ASCAP) and PEACH HILL SONGS (BMI)
Admin. by EMI CMG PUBLISHING
All Rights Reserved   Used by Permission

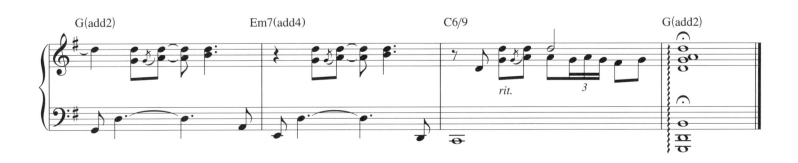

God Knew That I Needed You

Words and Music by
MEL TUNNEY

I Will Be Here

Words and Music by
STEVEN CURTIS CHAPMAN

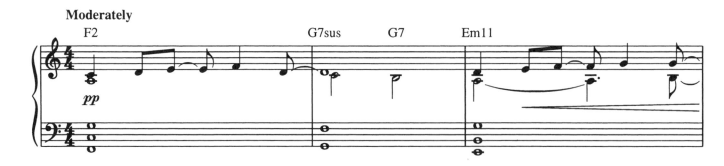

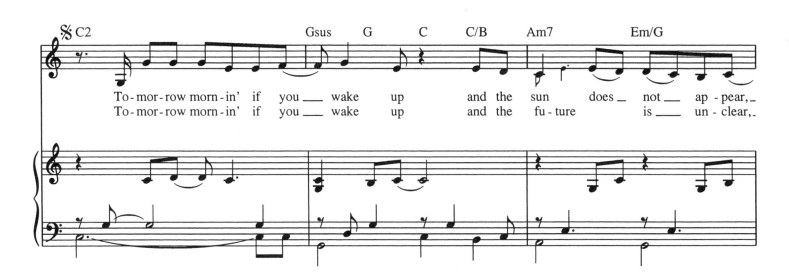

To-mor-row morn-in' if you __ wake up and the sun does __ not __ ap-pear, __
To-mor-row morn-in' if you __ wake up and the fu-ture is __ un-clear, __

© 1989, 1990 SPARROW SONG (BMI), GREG NELSON MUSIC (BMI) and UNIVERSAL MUSIC - CAREERS (BMI)
SPARROW SONG and GREG NELSON MUSIC Admin. by EMI CMG PUBLISHING
All Rights Reserved Used by Permission

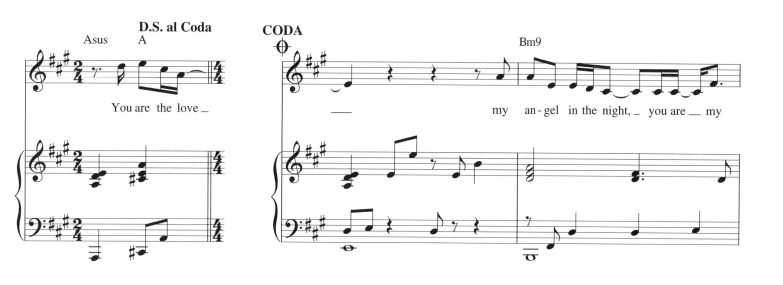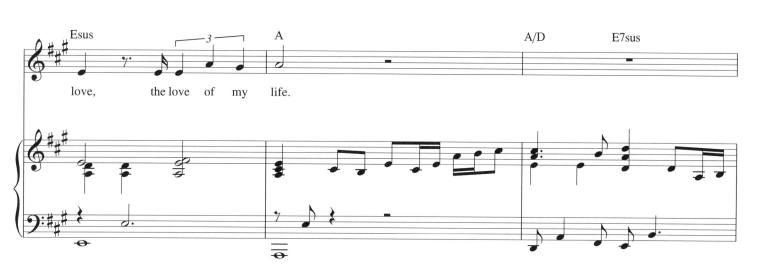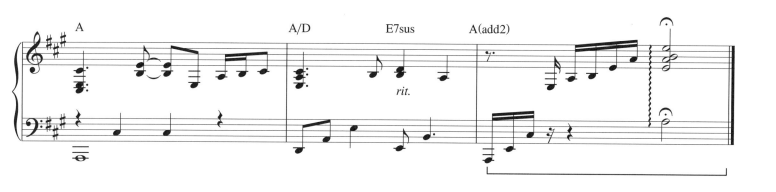

Love Will Be Our Home

Words and Music by
STEVEN CURTIS CHAPMAN

© 1988 SPARROW SONG (BMI), GREG NELSON MUSIC (BMI) and UNIVERSAL MUSIC - CAREERS (BMI)
SPARROW SONG and GREG NELSON MUSIC Admin. by EMI CMG PUBLISHING
All Rights Reserved   Used by Permission

*The ending either could be done loud or soft.

My Place Is With You

243

Words and Music by MICHAEL PURYEAR
and GEOFFREY THURMAN

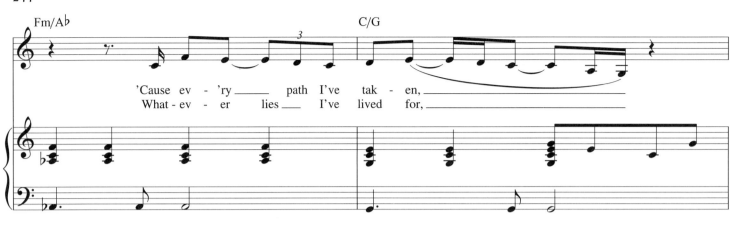

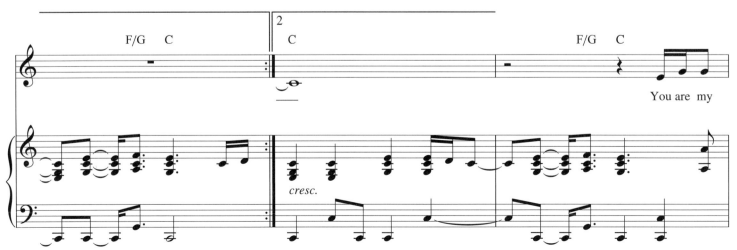

Shine On Us

Words and Music by MICHAEL W. SMITH
and DEBBIE SMITH

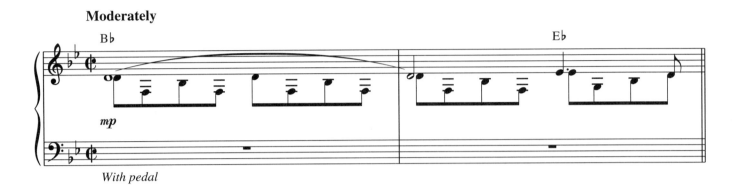

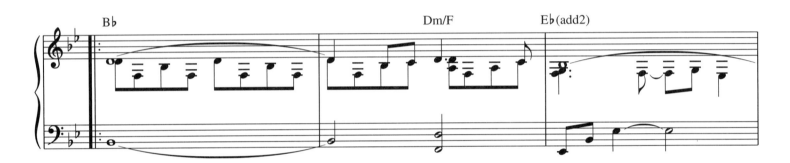

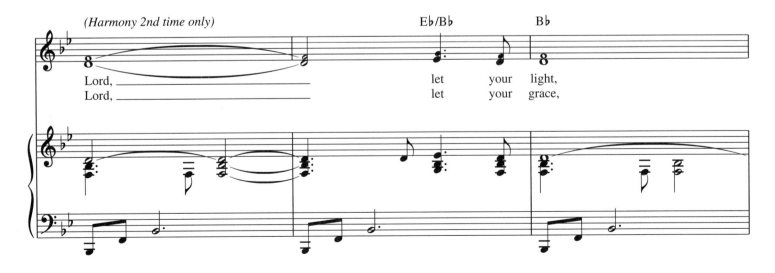

Lord, _____ let your light,
Lord, _____ let your grace,

Copyright © 1996 Sony/ATV Music Publishing LLC and Deer Valley Music
All Rights Administered by Sony/ATV Music Publishing LLC, 8 Music Square West, Nashville, TN 37203
International Copyright Secured   All Rights Reserved

Where There Is Love

Words and Music by PHILL McHUGH
and GREG NELSON

This Day

Words and Music by
LOWELL ALEXANDER

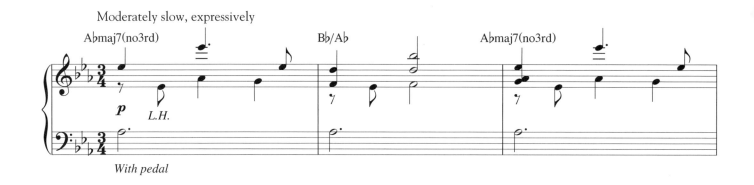
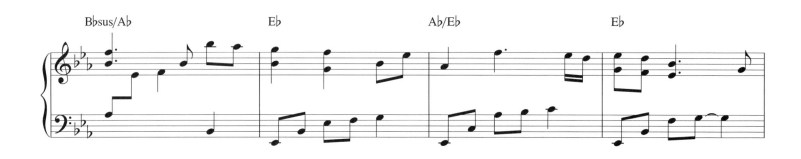
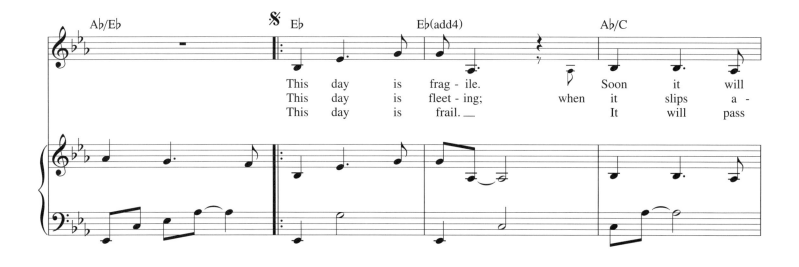

This day is frag-ile. Soon it will end, and once it has van-ished it will
This day is fleet-ing; when it slips a-way, not all our mon-ey can
This day is frail. It will pass by. So be-fore it's too late to re-

© 1993 MEADOWGREEN MUSIC COMPANY (ASCAP)
Admin. by EMI CMG PUBLISHING
All Rights Reserved   Used by Permission